MESSI'S FOOTBALL MIND GAME

Test Your Gaming Wisdom

By:
Alex Yurich

Welcome to our interactive soccer book! Here you can test your soccer knowledge and compete against Lionel Messi, one of the best soccer players of all time. You can also find yourself in Messi's game episodes and decide what you would do in his shoes. Maybe you would think the same way as him. Either way, it will be interesting and fun, and you can learn to be smarter at game thinking. Before we begin playing, let's discover some details about this remarkable player.

Messi was born in Rosario, Argentina to a working-class family. He was a small and thin youngster who enjoyed playing football with his brothers and friends on the street. His goal was to pursue a career as a professional footballer, following in the footsteps of his idol Diego Maradona. Sadly, at the age of 11, he was diagnosed with a rare illness that halted his growth. His folks couldn't afford the costly medical care, hence he put his dream of becoming a footballer in jeopardy.

But Messi kept practicing and playing soccer. He was so good that the scouts from Barcelona noticed him. They offered him a contract and helped pay for his medical treatment. At 13, Messi moved to Spain with his father while the rest of the family stayed in Argentina. It was tough because he missed his mom, siblings, and home country.

Messi started playing soccer for Barcelona's youth team. He was skilled and fast. He learned Spanish and the Catalan dialect so he could talk to his coaches and teammates. He went to school, but he wasn't really interested in his studies. Soccer was his true passion. When he was 16, he played his first game for Barcelona's top team and scored a goal in the Spanish championship. He became the youngest player in the club's history to do so.

Since then, Messi became one of the top soccer players globally. He won several championships and accolades with his club and the Argentine national team. Messi scored over 700 career goals and broke many records. He received the Ballon d'Or 7 times, which is the most renowned individual soccer award. He also inspired millions of children as a role model. In 2022, Messi led Argentina to victory in the World Cup.

Messi excels not only in soccer but also in character. He is modest, compassionate, and magnanimous. At the age of 9, he met Antonella Rocuzzo, his childhood friend who is now his wife. They have three sons: Thiago, Mateo, and Ciro. Messi cherishes family time and spends all his free time with them. He also assists those in need through his Lionel Messi Charitable Foundation, which backs education, health, and sports initiatives for young people in Argentina and other nations.

In this book, you can challenge yourself and test your soccer knowledge against Lionel Messi. Are you prepared for this challenge? If the answer is yes, then let's begin!

The game is easy. You'll see a clip of Lionel Messi playing, with or without the ball. You'll be presented with two or three potential outcomes. Choose the correct one and provide an explanation. Better yet, write it down.

After you choose the future situation on the field, we will explain all the options and why each one earns a certain number of points. Guess what Messi will do and get a bonus.

Our game has 7 rounds. Complete all 7 rounds, and we calculate your total score and Messi's. Then, we compare scores to see who has more. Make sure to follow the rules and play fair.

The top choice earns three points, while the next best is worth two points.

Messi's pick is worth one point, and an incorrect option earns zero points.

Choosing the best and Messi's options together earns five points.

Here's a game example.

Imagine I'm Alex and I'm starting in the first round.

Examine the picture closely. Analyze the field's situation and note the locations of Messi, his teammates, and the opposing team. Where are the opponents? ball at the centeof the opponent's penalty area. What can he do to attack?

Examine the picture closely. Analyze the field's situation and note the locations of Messi, his teammates, and the opposing team. Where are the opponents?

Examine the picture closely. Analyze the field's situation and note the locations of Messi, his teammates, and the opposing team. Where are the opponents?

Option A. Messi can pass to a player entering the penalty area.

Why did you choose Option A?

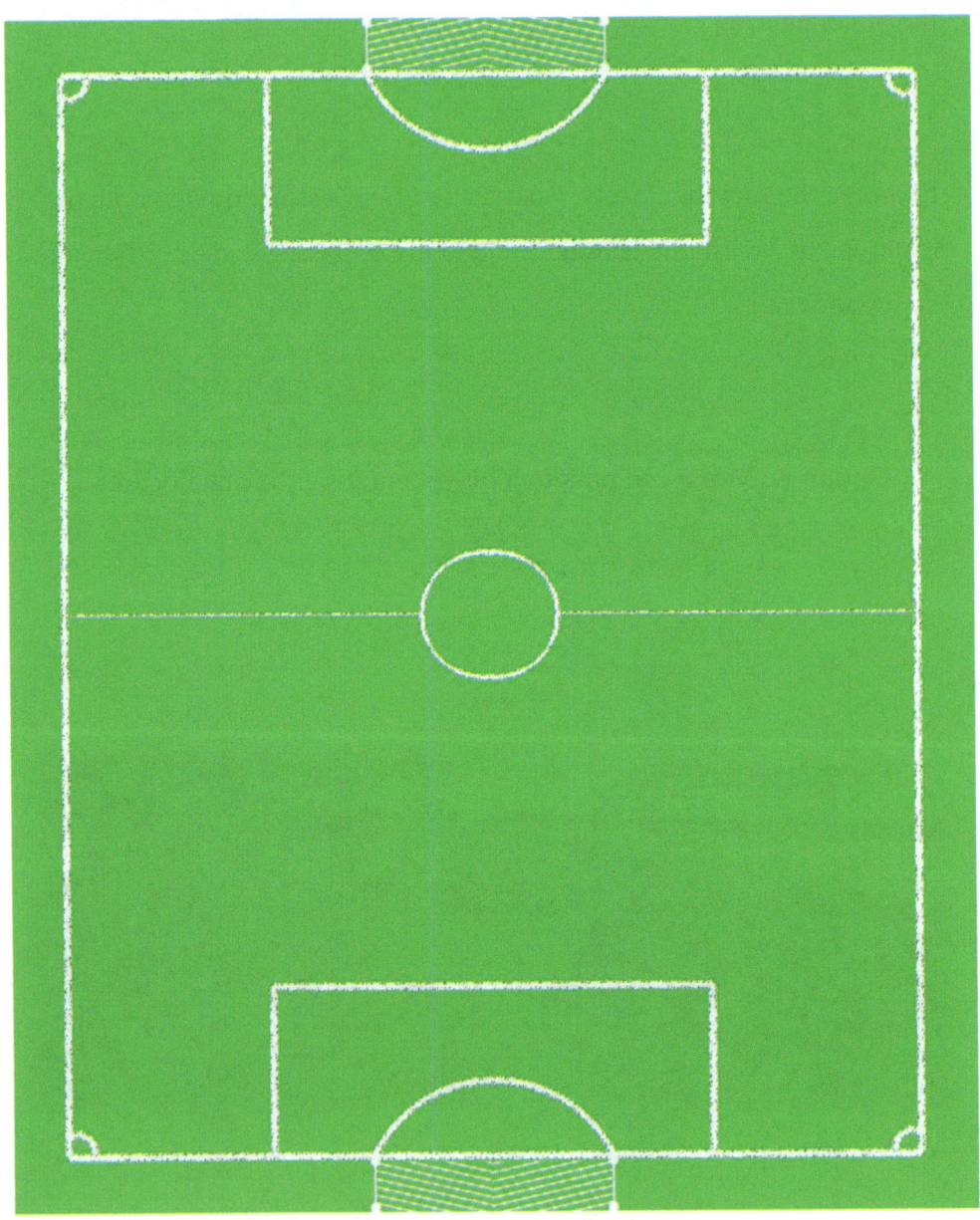

Option B. Messi can take a long-range shot on goal.

Why did you choose Option B?

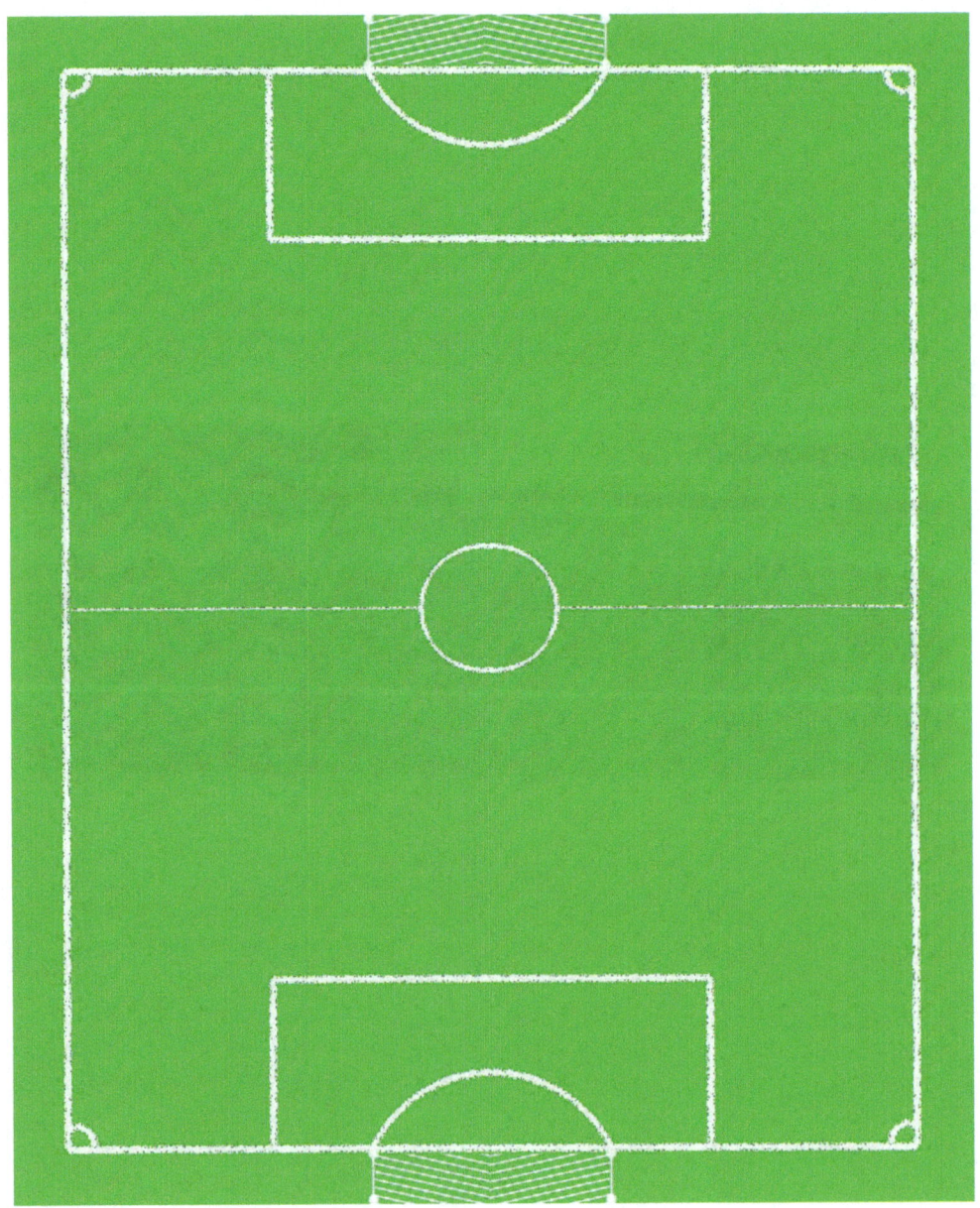

Option C. Messi can pass to the advancing player on the left in the space available.

Why did you choose Option C?

I choose this option because with this pass you can put a player on the left in a very dangerous shooting position.

The best option - 3 points.

The second option, also good - 2 points.

Guessed Messi's option - 1 point.

Inappropriate option - 0 points.

The best option + Messi's option - 5 points.

Summarize the results.

Option A. Good option, but difficult. The space between the defenders where you can pass is very narrow. And you have to pass in time so that the player does not have time to run offside. This option - 2 points.

Option B. Not a good option. Long shot. Two defenders meet Messi with the ball and cover the angle of the shot. There are better ways to develop the attack. This option is worth 0 points.

Option C. Good option. The player on the left is in a good position to get into a dangerous position for a shot. This option is worth 3 points.

What Lionel Messi chose?

Messi chose the best option. He decided to pass to the player on the left. And put him in a dangerous shooting position. If you choose this option, you get 5 points. Best option + option

Messi himself gets 3 points. He chose the best option.

After the 1st round we count the points.

Alex VS Lionel Messi

Players	Alex	Messi
1 round	5 points	3 points
2 round		
3 round		
4 round		
5 round		
6 round		
7 round		
Bottom line		

I hope you've learned the rules of the game from our example with Alex. Now you can start! I wish you good luck!

FIRST TOUR.

Lionel Messi has the ball in the middle of the pitch. What attacking options does he have?

Look at the picture carefully. Think, evaluate the situation on the field. Where is Messi himself? Where are the teammates? Where are the opponents?

Option A. Leo can pass to the left, to partner #2.

Why did you choose this option A?

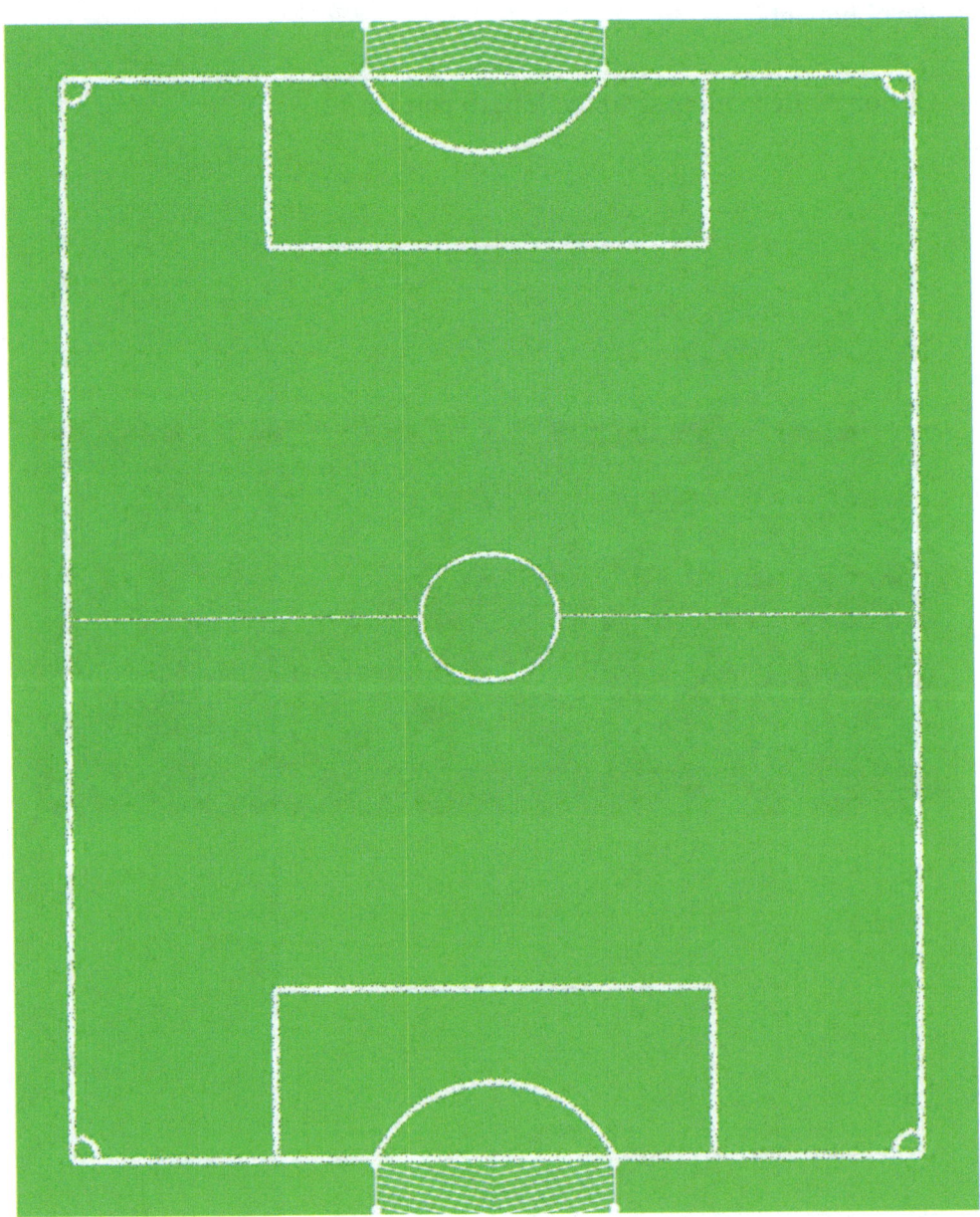

Option B. Leo can pass forward to a partner in the middle.

Why did you choose Option B?

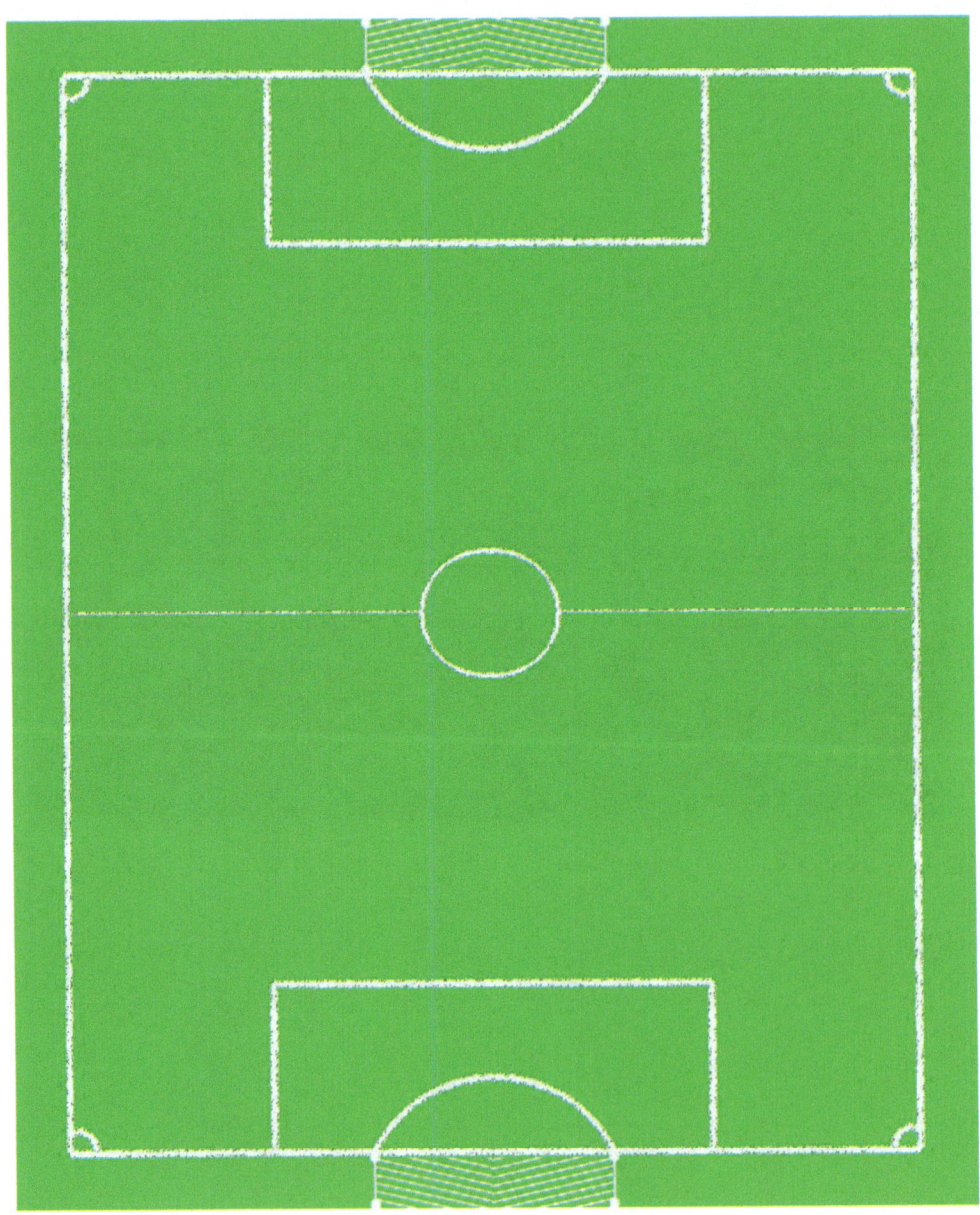

Option C. Messi can play a through ball behind the defenders.

Why did you choose Option C?

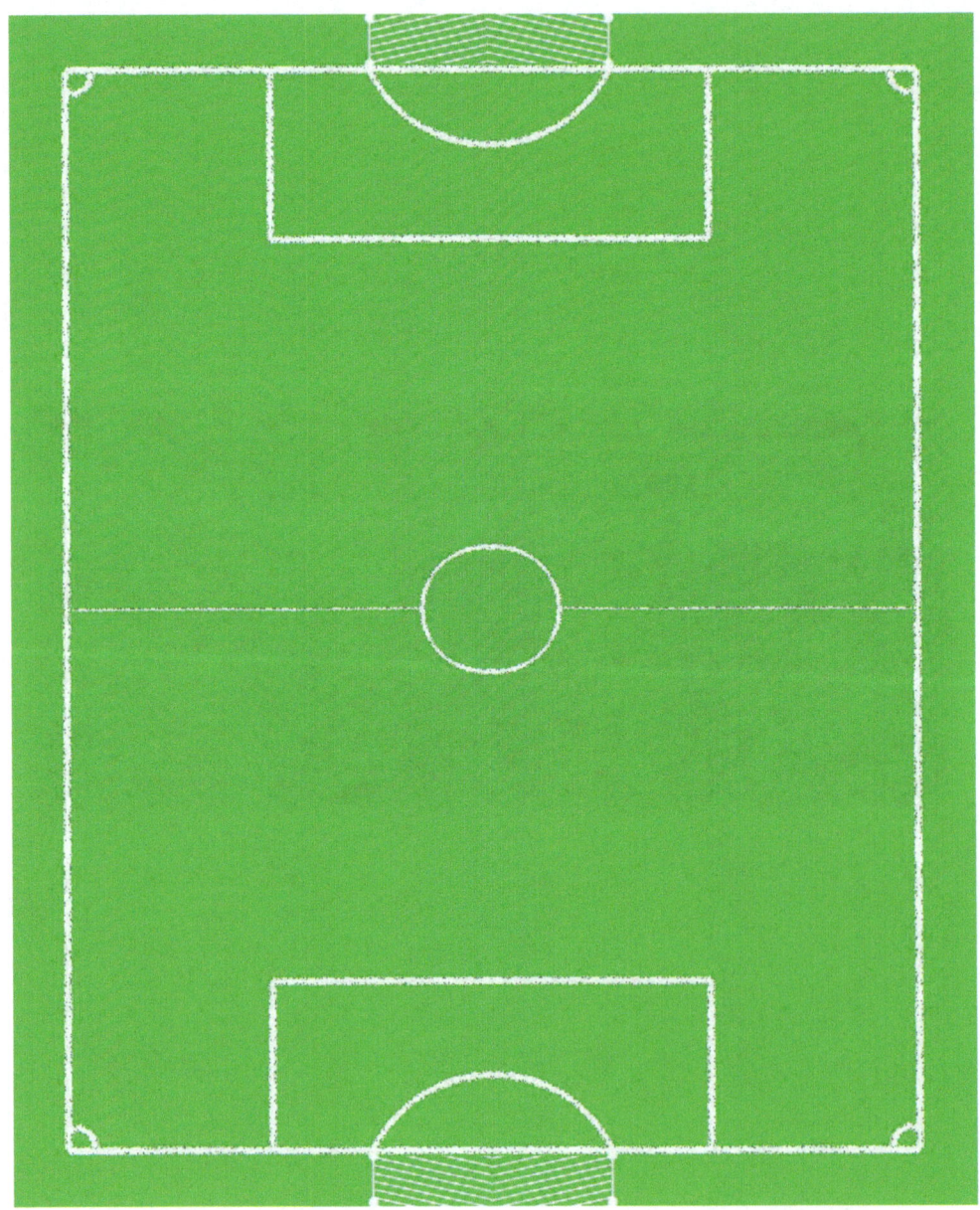

The best option - 3 points.

The second option, also good - 2 points.

Guessed Messi option - 1 point.

Inappropriate option - 0 points.

The best option + Messi option - 5 points.

Let's summarize the results.

Option A. Good variation. Pass to develop a quick attack. This variation-2 points.

Option B. Good variation. Forward pass to develop a quick attack. This variation - 2 points.

Option C. The best option. There is a pass line to pass to the running player behind the defenders into the open space. This option - 3 points.

What did Lionel Messi choose?

We can see that Messi has chosen the best option. By choosing this option you get - 5 points. You have chosen the best option and also guessed Leo's decision.

Messi himself gets 3 points. He chose the best option.

After the first round, we'll add up the points.

AGAINST

VS Lionel Messi

Players		Lionel Messi
1 round		3 points
2 round		
3 round		
4 round		
5 round		
6 round		
7 round		
Bottom line		

SECOND ROUND.

Lionel Messi has the ball. What are his attacking options?

Look at the picture carefully. Think, evaluate the situation on the field. Where is Messi himself? Where are the teammates? Where are the opponents?

Option A. Leo can pass to the feet of player #2.

Why did you choose Option A?

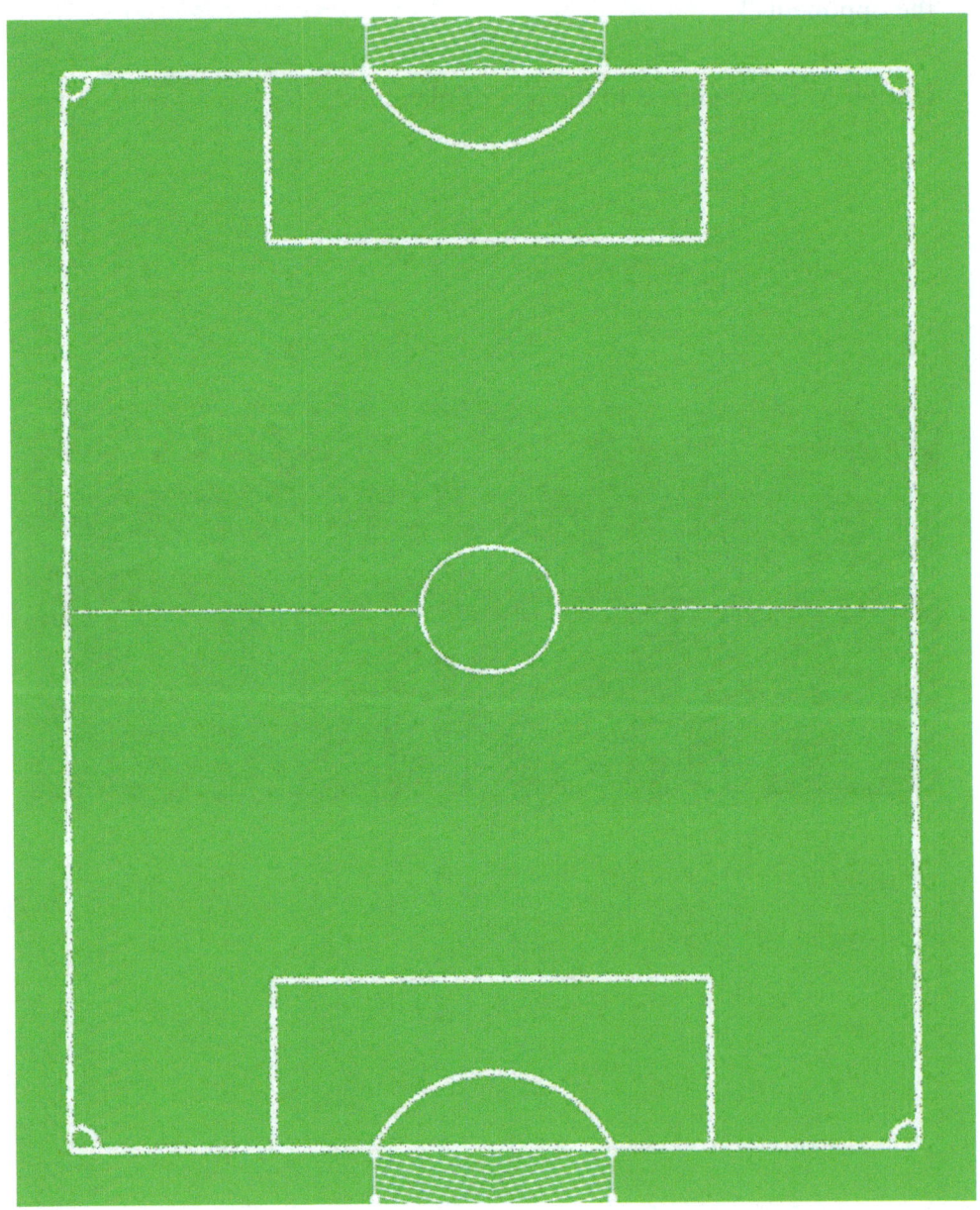

Option B. Messi passes the ball behind the back of the opposing fullback to an open partner.

Why did you choose Option B?

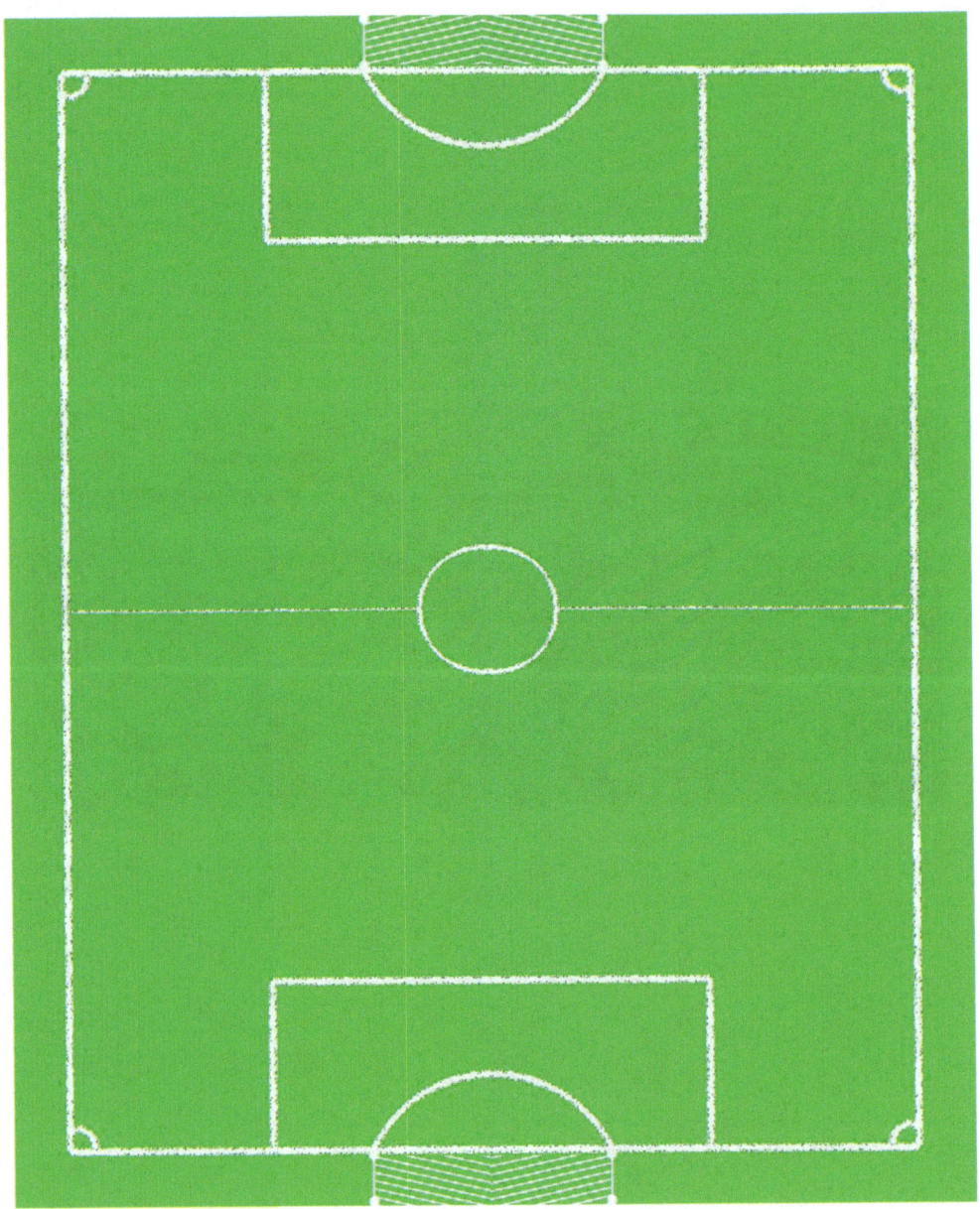

The best option - 3 points.

The second option, also good - 2 points.

Guessed Messi option - 1 point.

Inappropriate option - 0 points.

The best option + Messi option - 5 points.

Let's summarize the results.

Variation A. After passing to a partner, the player has his back to the opponent's goal and is under pressure from the opponent. This variation scores 0 points.

Option B. The best option for quick progress. Where are goals scored? That's right, at the other team's goal. You need the shortest route. Here it is. By freeing up your partner on the right, who actively enters the space behind the defender. That's three points.

What did Lionel Messi choose?

Leo chose option A. And as you can see in the photo, the partner who received the ball was under pressure, with his back to the goal. If you choose this option, you get 0 points.

Messi himself gets 0 points.

After the second round, we'll add up the points.

VS Lionel Messi

Players		Lionel Messi
1 round		3 points
2 round		0 points
3 round		
4 round		
5 round		
6 round		
7 round		
Bottom line		

You're doing great! It's been two rounds of our championship. Here's a bonus. Interesting fact about Lionel Messi.

Messi signed his first professional contract with Barcelona on a napkin because a club representative didn't have paper. The contract was signed in 2000, when Messi was 13 years old.

THIRD ROUND.

Lionel Messi without the ball. What are his options?

Look at the picture carefully. Think, evaluate the situation on the field. Where is Messi himself? Where are the teammates? Where are the opponents?

Option A. Lionel can stay in the area highlighted in the photo and receive a pass to his feet.

Why did you choose Option A?

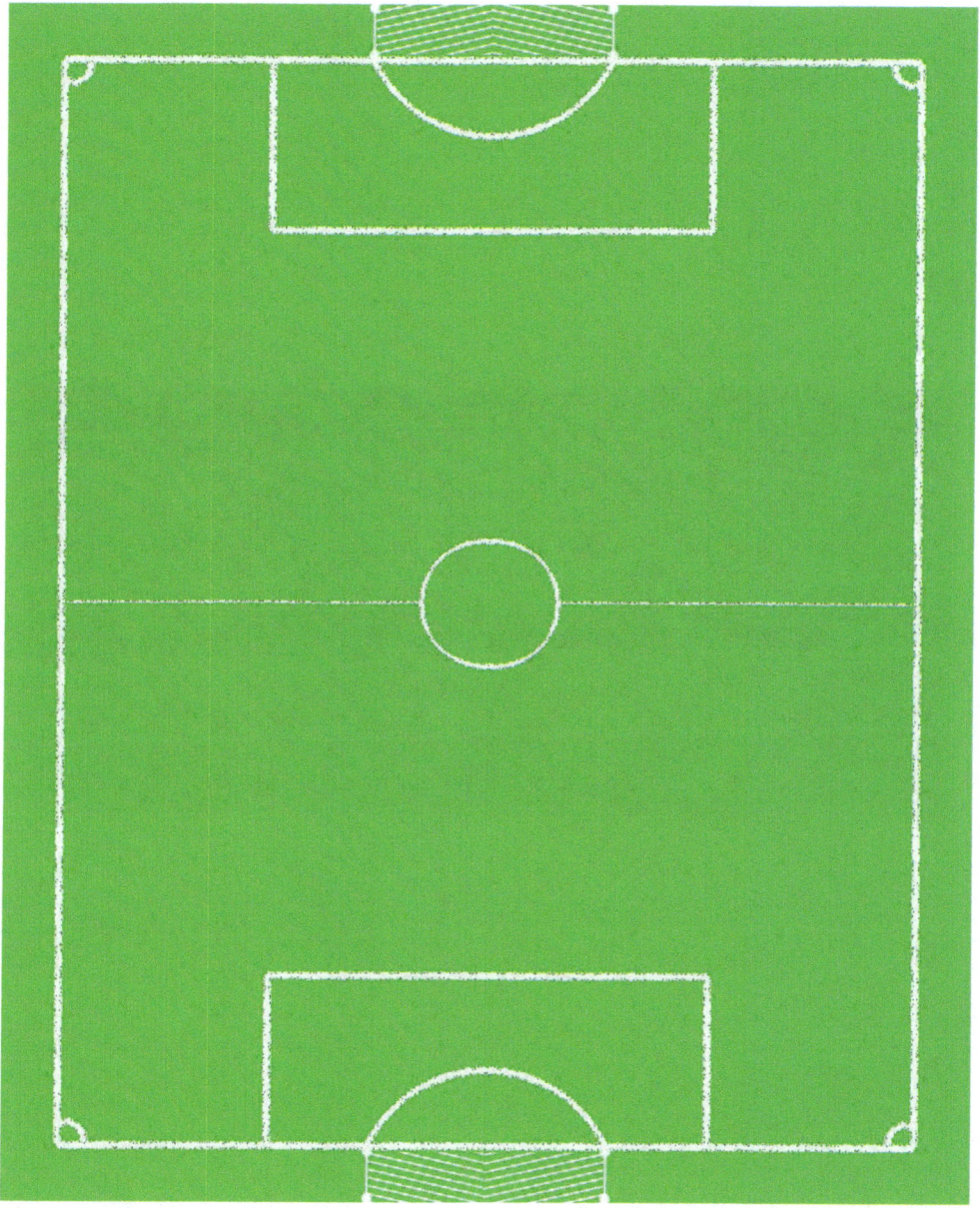

Option B. Messi can make a fast break behind the defenders into open space.

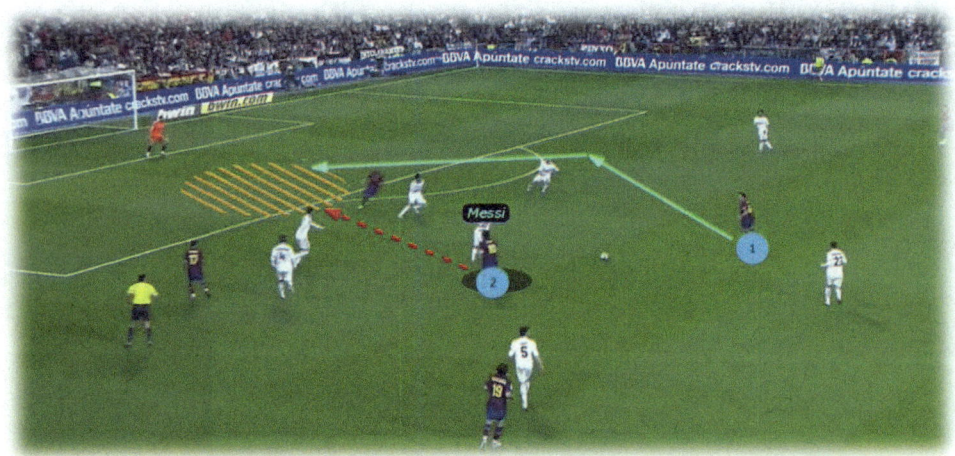

Why did you choose Option B?

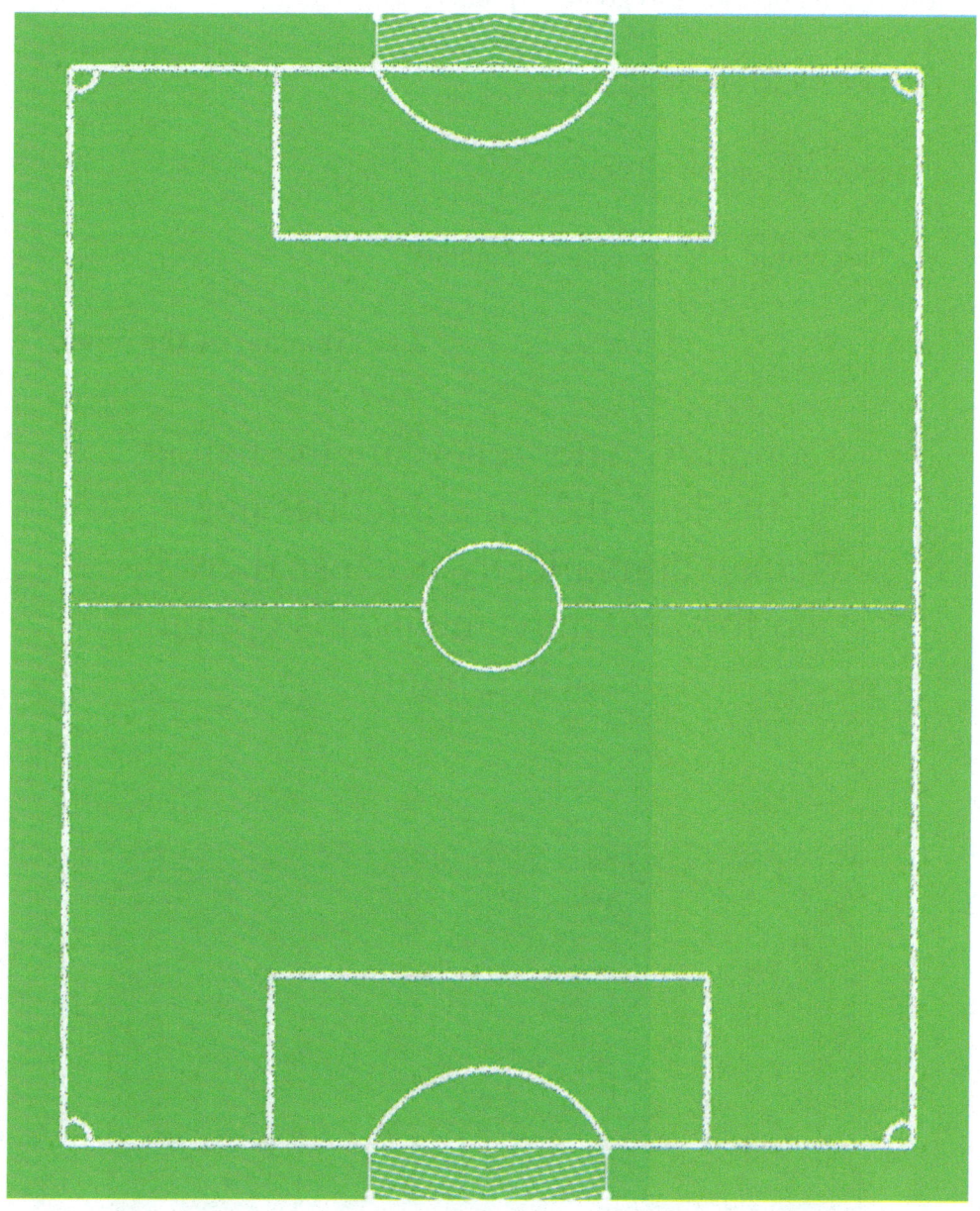

The best option - 3 points.

The second option, also good - 2 points.

Guessed Messi option - 1 point.

Inappropriate option - 0 points.

The best option + Messi option - 5 points.

Let's summarize the results.

Option A. After receiving the ball at the feet, the situation does not change dramatically because there is no forward movement. This option scores 2 points.

Option B. Very good option. Open up into the open space behind the backs of the defenders. You only need a timely pass. This option 3 points.

What did Lionel Messi choose?

We see Messi bursting into the penalty area and receiving a well-timed pass. He scored a beautiful goal. By choosing this option you get - 5 points. You chose the best option and you also guessed Lionel's decision.

Messi himself gets 3 points. He chose the best option.

VS Lionel Messi

Players		Lionel Messi
1 round		3 points
2 round		2 points
3 round		3 points
4 round		
5 round		
6 round		
7 round		
Bottom line		

FOURTH ROUND.

Lionel Messi has the ball in the penalty area. What attacking options does he have?

Look at the picture carefully. Think, evaluate the situation on the field. Where is Messi himself? Where are the teammates? Where are the opponents?

Option A. Messi can shoot from an acute angle.

Why did you choose Option A?

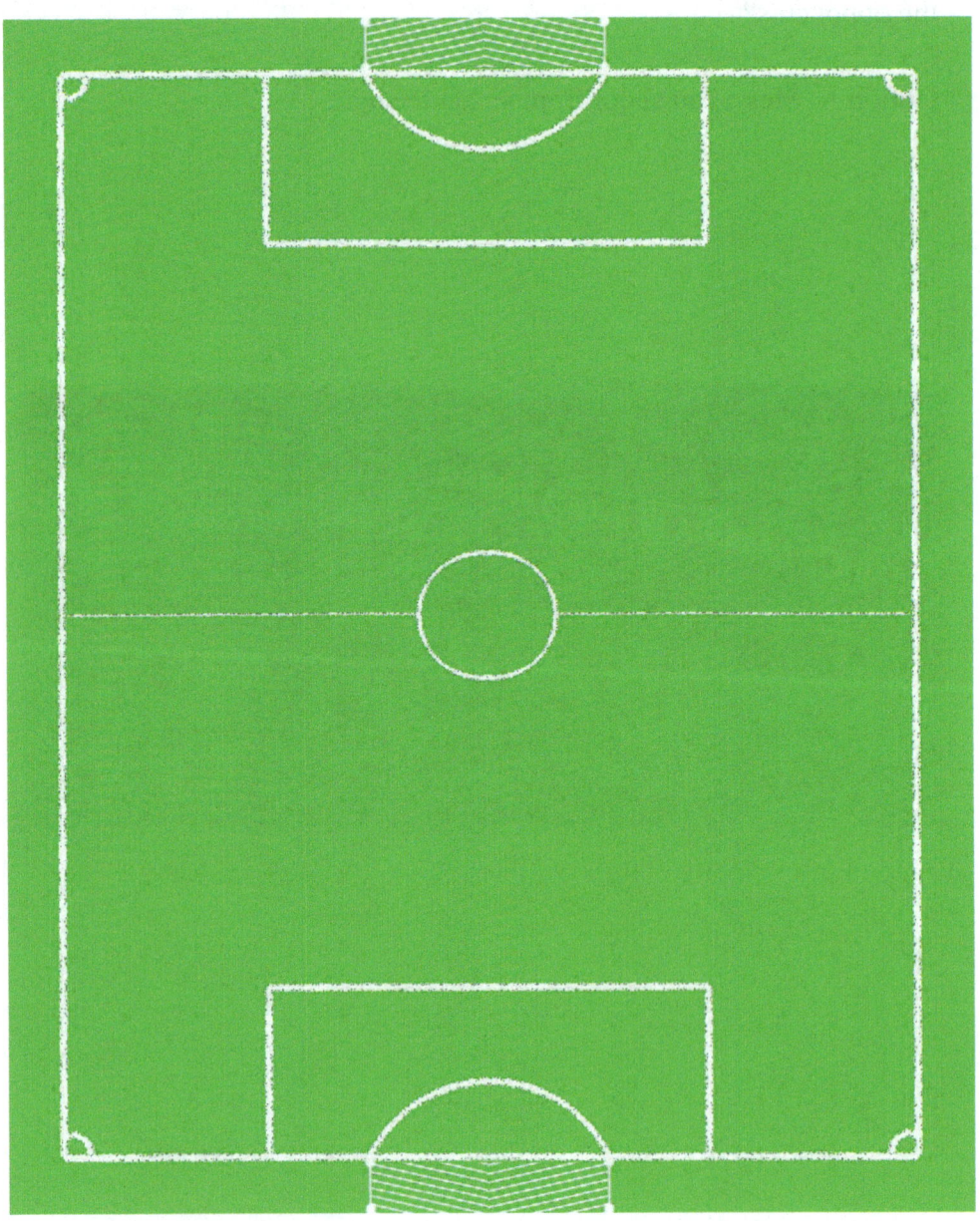

Option B. Messi can pass to a nearby player for a shot.

Why did you choose this option B?

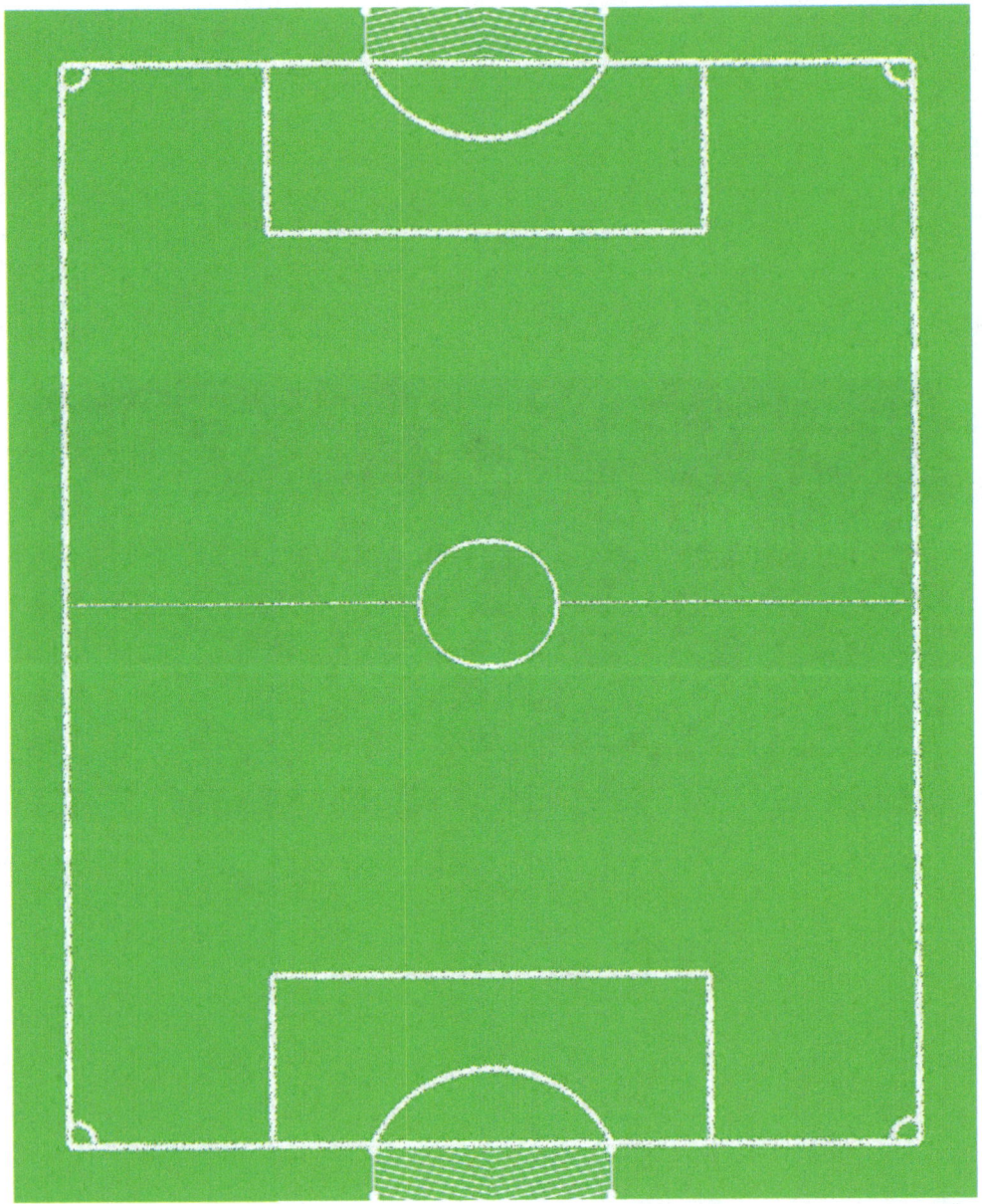

Option C. Lionel can pass to a long distance player for a second step.

Why did you choose Option C?

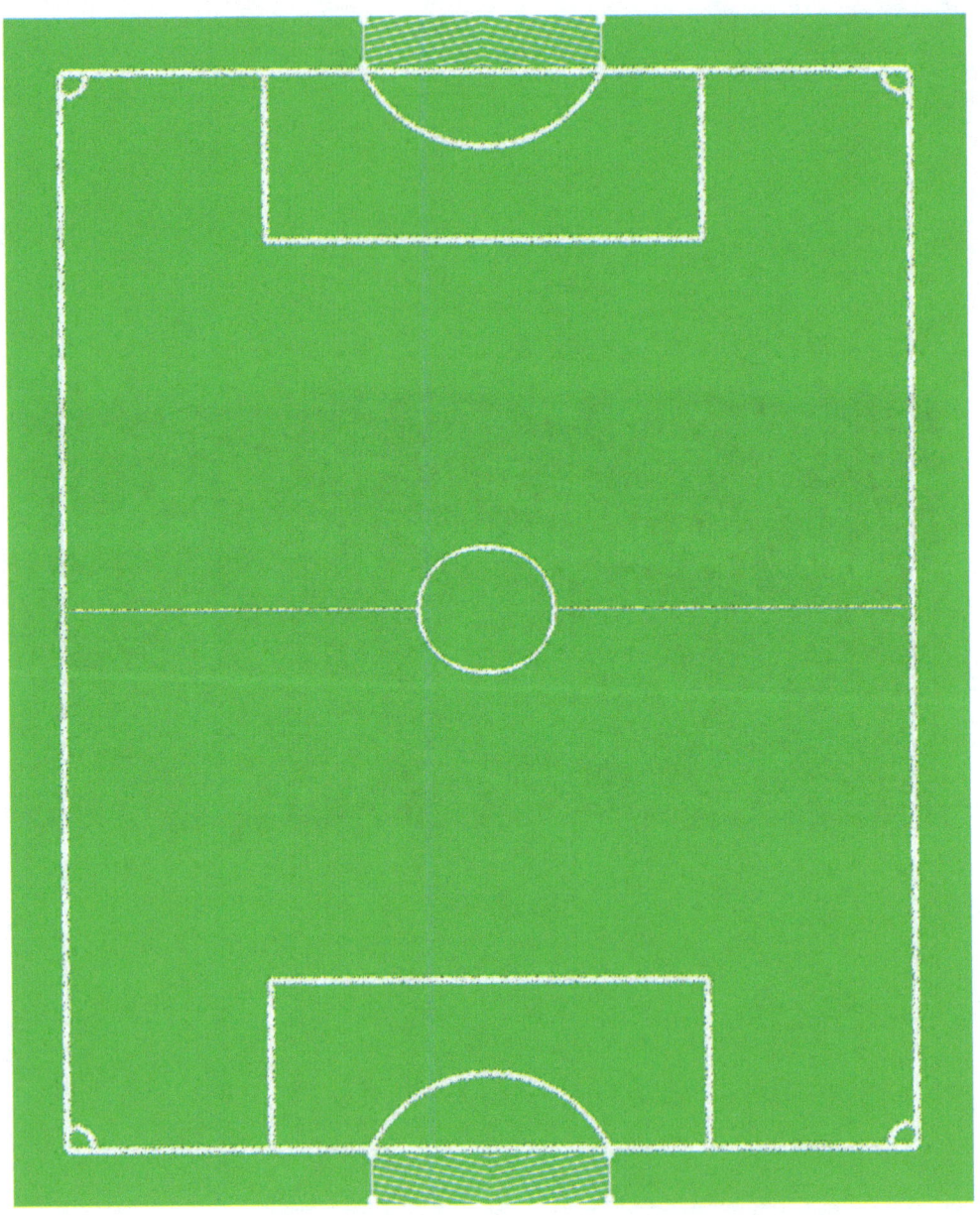

The best option - 3 points.

The second option, also good - 2 points.

Guessed Messi option - 1 point.

Inappropriate option - 0 points.

The best option + Messi option - 5 points.

Let's summarize the results.

Option A. Not the best option. It's a sharp angle for the shot. Messi has the goalkeeper and defender in front of him. The angle of the shot is too low. There are better and more correct ways to score a goal. This option - 0 points.

Option B. Passing to a close player is a good option. But the defender is too close and has the opportunity to intercept the pass. This option is worth 2 points.

Option C. The best option is to pass to the outside player, under the second tempo. This variant 3 points.

What did Lionel Messi choose?

We can see that Messi passed to the far post and then the ball was scored. By choosing this option you get - 5 points. You have chosen the best option and you have also guessed Lionel's decision.

Messi himself gets 3 points. He chose the best option.

After the first round, we'll add up the points.

VS Lionel Messi

Players		Lionel Messi
1 round		3 points
2 round		2 points
3 round		3 points
4 round		3 points
5 round		
6 round		
7 round		
Bottom line		

You're doing great! It's been four rounds of our championship. Here's a bonus. Interesting fact about Lionel Messi.

Messi is the youngest player to be nominated for the Ballon d'Or, the prestigious award given to the best footballer of the year. He was 19 when he received his first nomination in 2006.

FIFTH TOUR.

Lionel Messi has the ball in the middle of the pitch. What are his attacking options?

Look at the picture carefully. Think, evaluate the situation on the field. Where is Messi himself? Where are the teammates? Where are the opponents?

Option A. Messi can pass to the player on the right. Внимательно посмотри на картинку.

Why did you choose Option A?

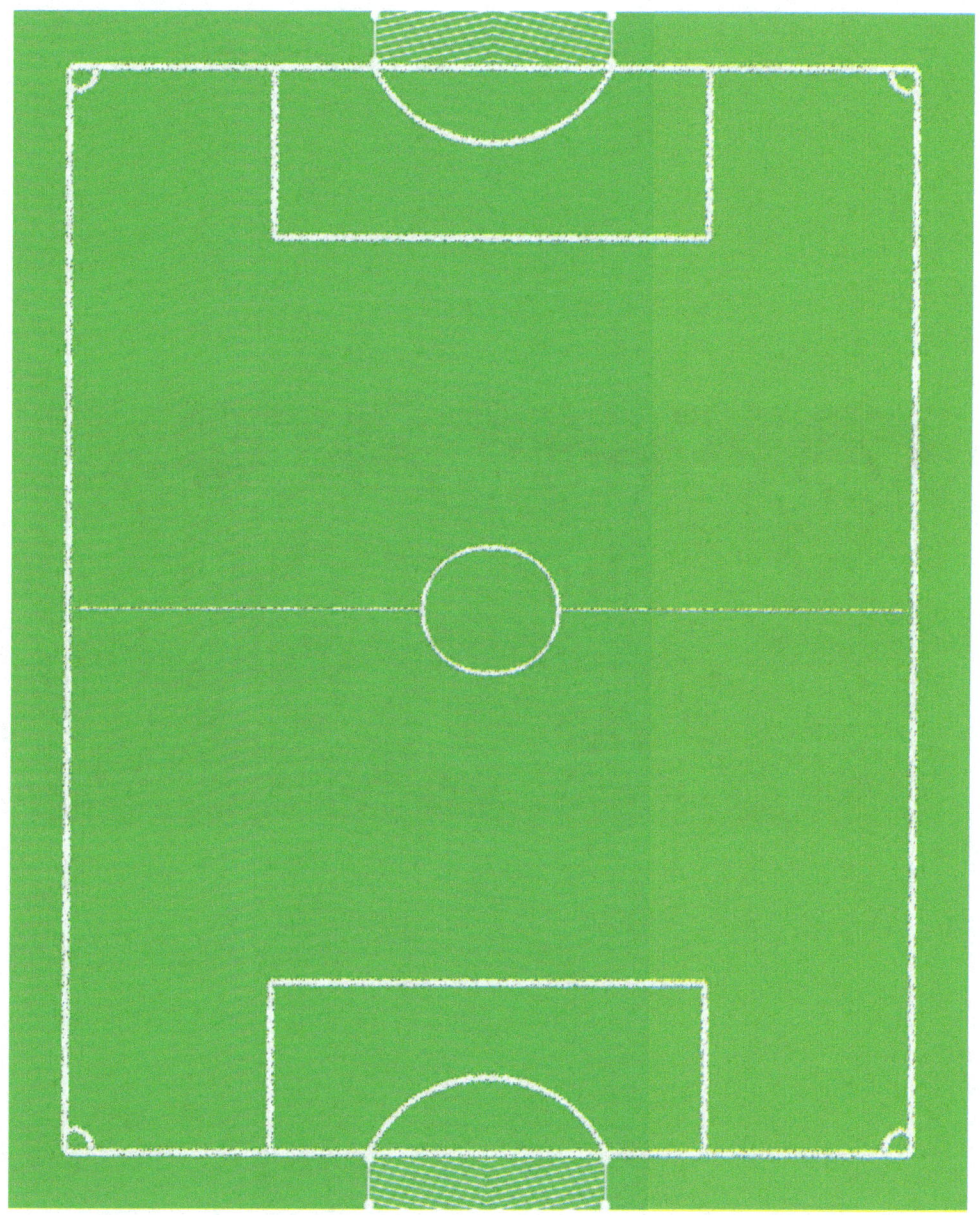

Option B. Messi can pass to his left.

Why did you choose Option B?

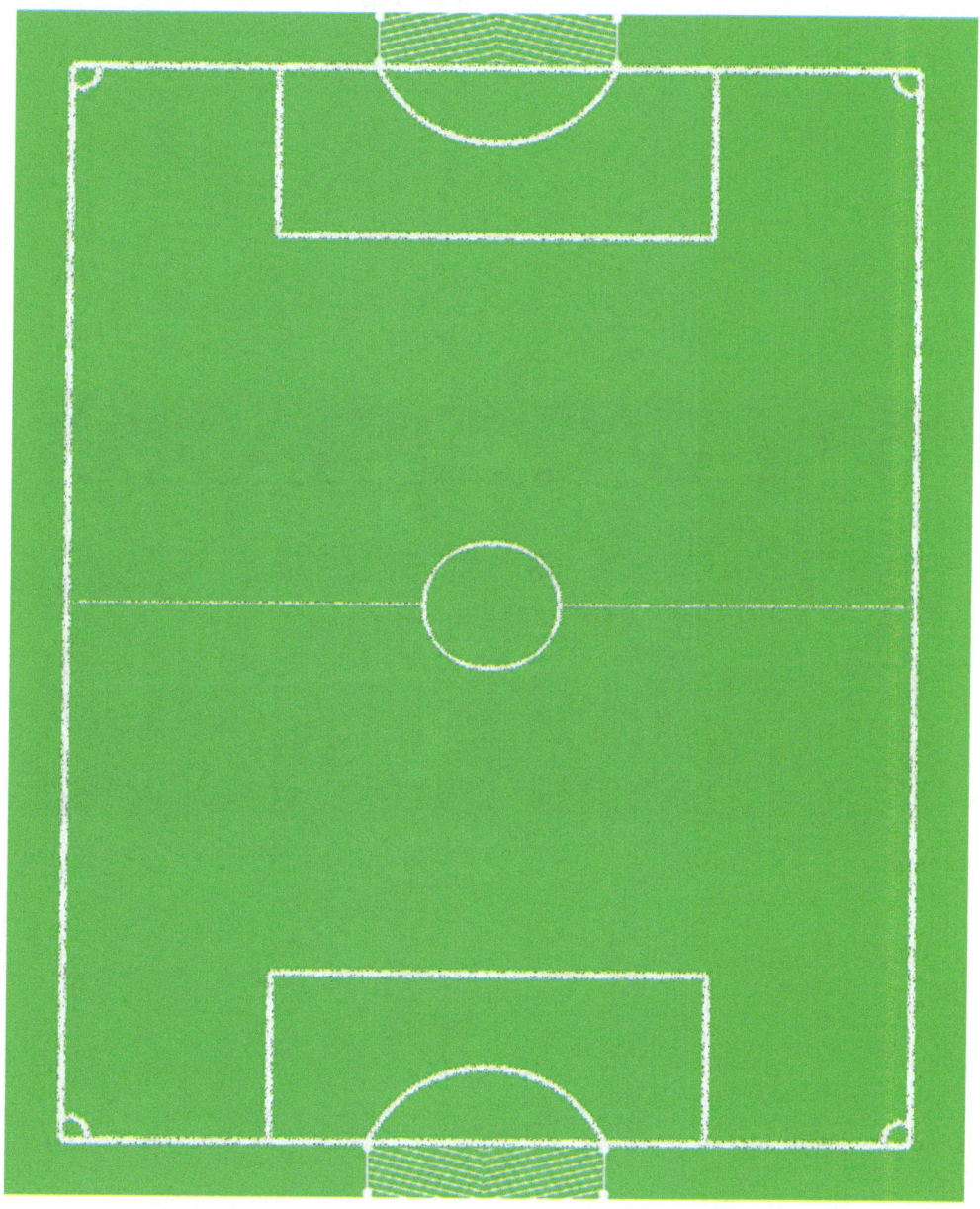

Option C. Messi can continue to pass the ball to an opponent.

Why did you choose Option C?

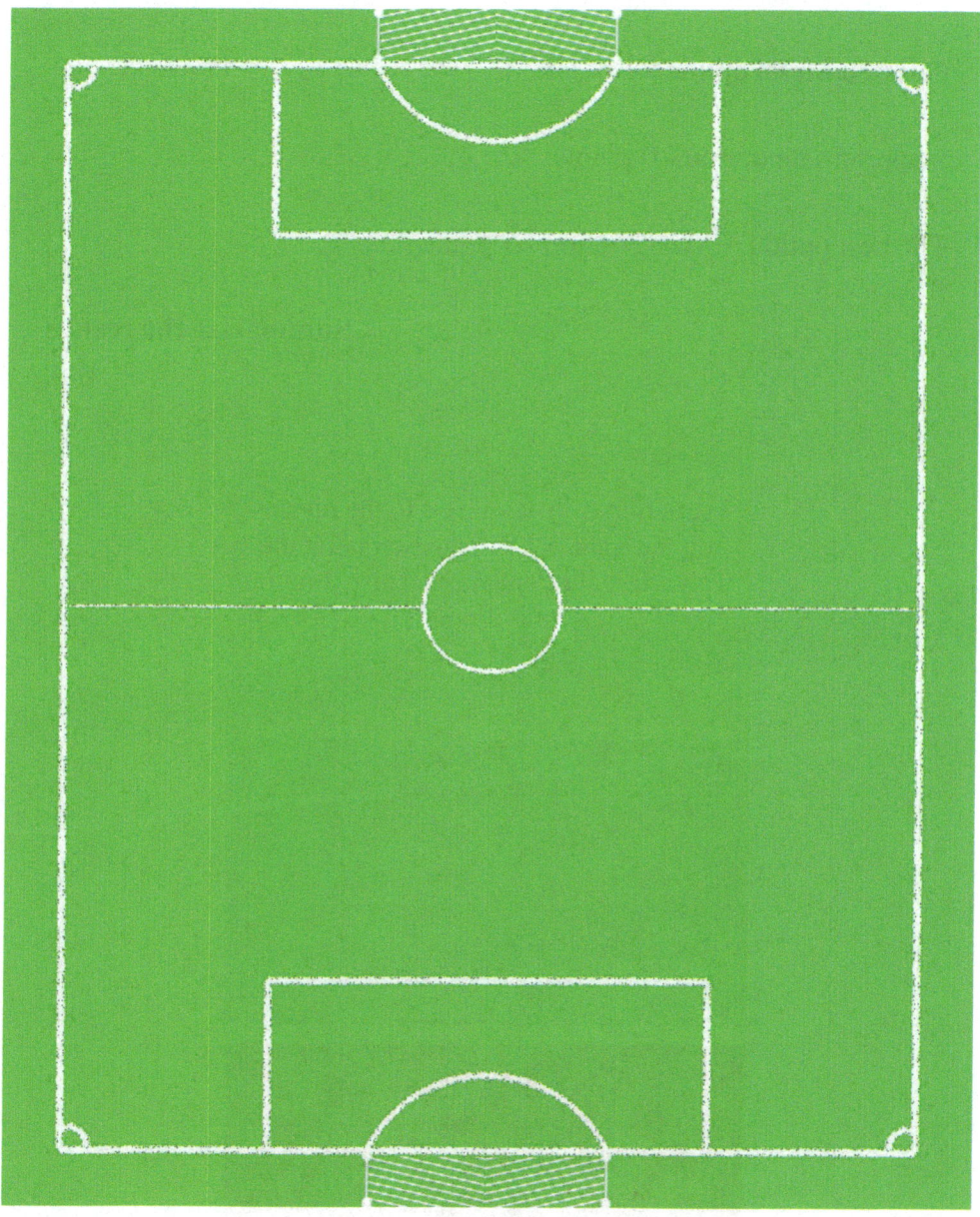

The best option - 3 points.

The second option, also good - 2 points.

Guessed Messi option - 1 point.

Inappropriate option - 0 points.

The best option + Messi option - 5 points.

Summarize the results.

Variation A. After a pass to the player on the right, a 1X1 situation is set up with a fast attack at speed. This variation scores 2 points.

Option B. The most promising option is to pass to the left to a player running into the box at speed. This option is worth 3 points.

Option C. Not the best option. There are players in a better position. If Messi continues with the ball, the player on the left is already offside. This option scores 0 points.

What did Lionel Messi choose?

Messi chose the wrong option. He could have played a pass to put a player in a dangerous position. But he ended up losing the ball. If you choose this option, you get 1 point. You guessed Leo's decision.

Messi himself gets 0 points. He didn't choose the best option.

After the fifth round, we'll add up the points.

VS Lionel Messi

Players		Lionel Messi
1 round		3 points
2 round		2 points
3 round		3 points
4 round		3 points
5 round		0 points
6 round		
7 round		
Bottom line		

SIXTH TOUR.

Lionel Messi with the ball. What are his attacking options?

Look at the picture carefully. Think, evaluate the situation on the field. Where is Messi himself? Where are the teammates? Where are the opponents?

Option A. Messi can make a pass to player #2, who has bounced under the pass.

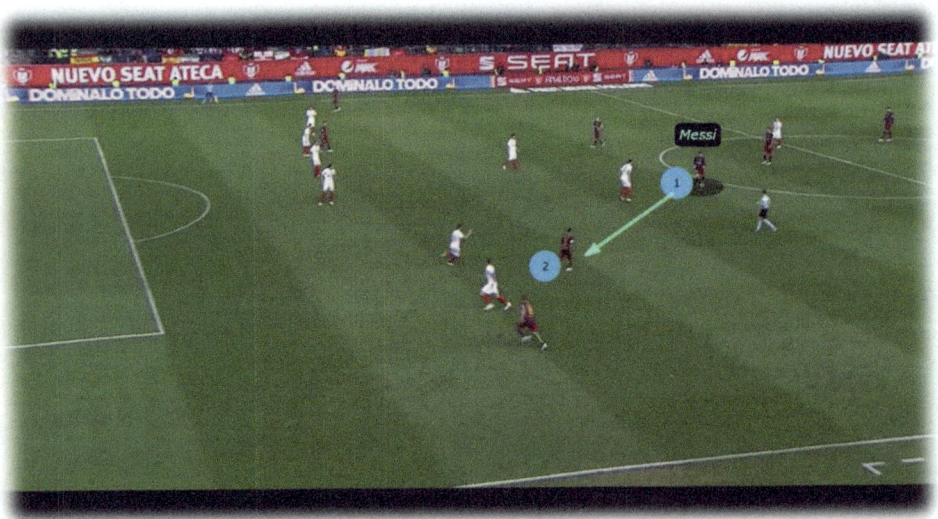

Why did you choose Option A?

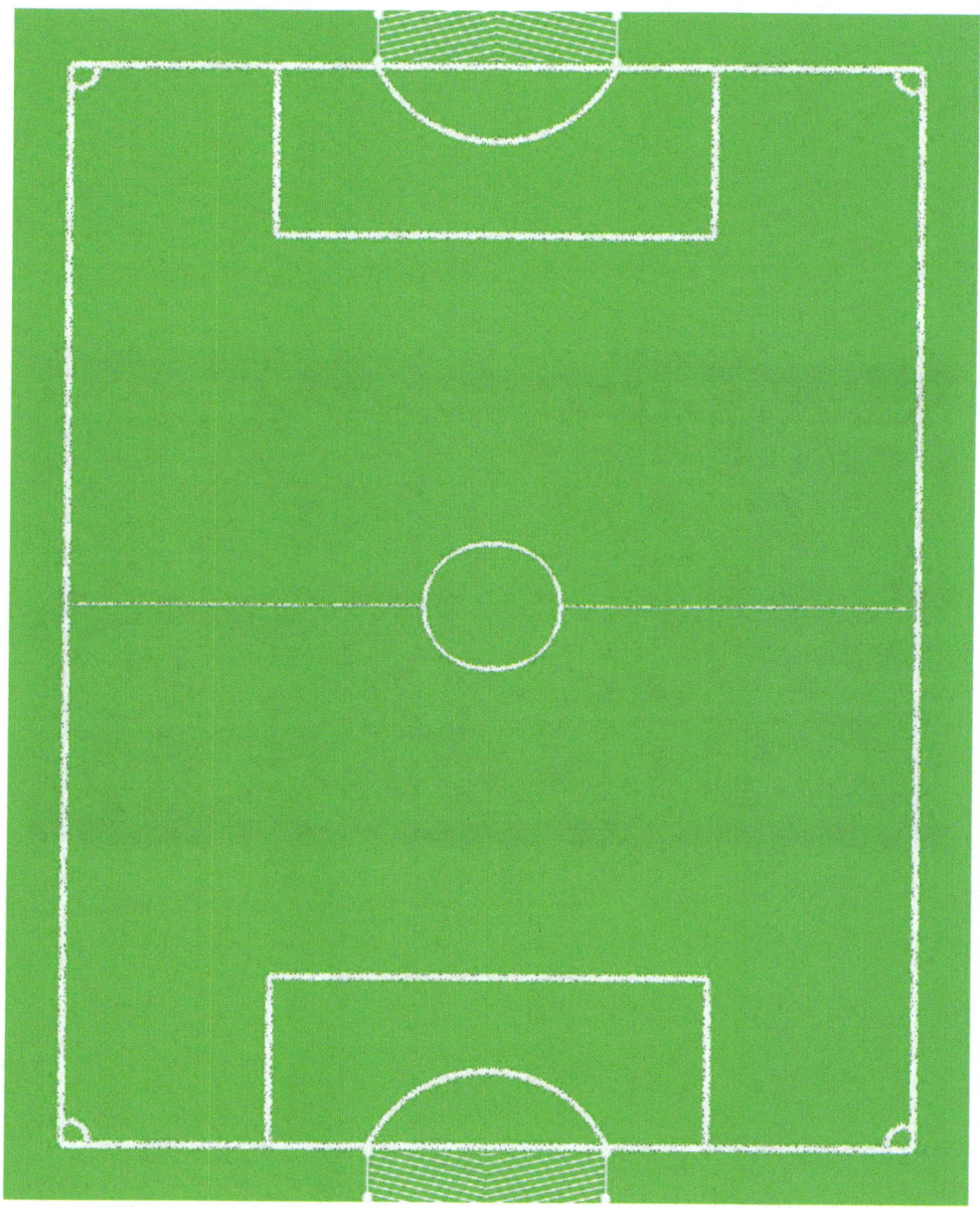

Option B. Messi plays a high pass behind the defenders to a running #2.

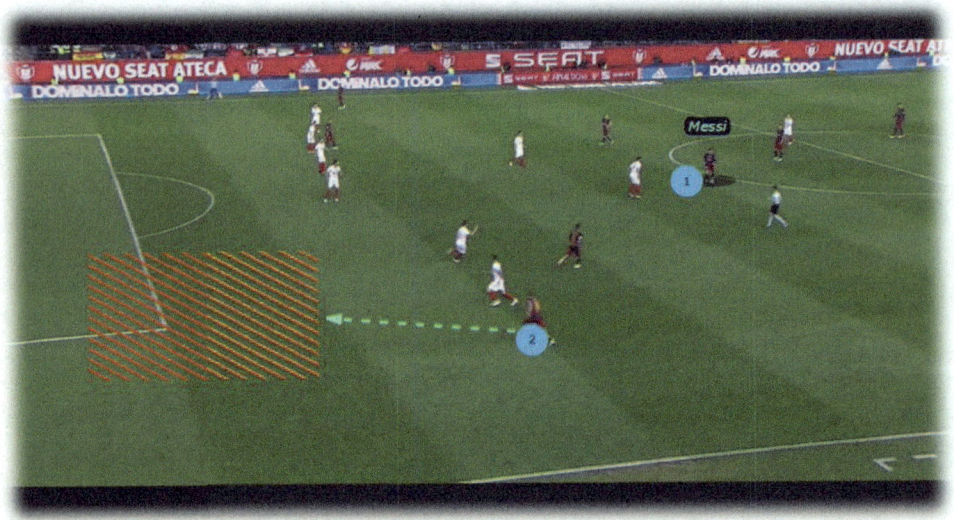

Why did you choose this option B?

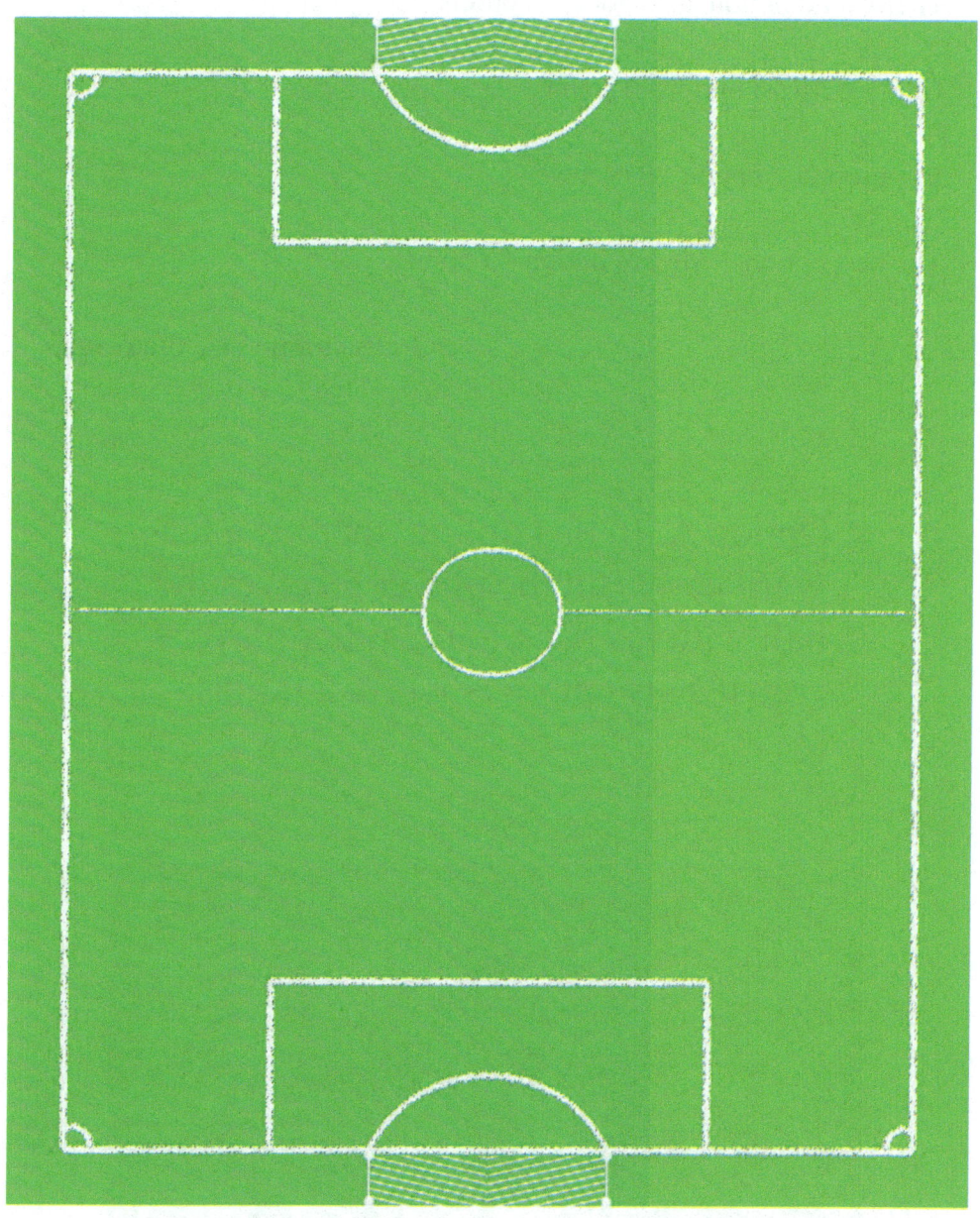

The best option - 3 points.

The second option, also good - 2 points.

Guessed Messi option - 1 point.

Inappropriate option - 0 points.

The best option + Messi's option - 5 points.

Let's summarize the results.

Option A. In this option, there is a forward pass. But the player receives the ball with his back to the other player's goal. This option is worth 2 points.

Option B. The best option. It is necessary to make a timely and accurate pass behind the back. This option scores 3 points.

What did Lionel Messi choose?

Messi chose a difficult but promising option. After Leo's pass, a goal was scored. For choosing this option you get -5 points. You chose the best option and you also guessed Lionel's decision.

Messi himself gets 3 points. He chose the best option.

VS Lionel Messi

Players		Lionel Messi
1 round		3 points
2 round		2 points
3 round		3 points
4 round		0 points
5 round		3 points
6 round		3 points
7 round		
Bottom line		

You're doing great! Two more rounds of our championship. Here's your bonus. Fun facts about Lionel Messi.

Messi loves to play video games, especially soccer simulators like FIFA and Pro Evolution Soccer. He has also appeared on the cover of these games several times.

SEVENTH ROUND.

The seventh round is final and special. Here we will test your intuition. You have to guess whether Lionel Messi will score a goal or not.

Your correct answer is worth 3 points.

Your wrong answer is worth 0 points.

If Messi scores, he gets - 3 points.

If Messi doesn't score, he gets - 0 points.

If you got the answer right and Lionel didn't score, you get -6 points.

Lionel Messi is preparing to take a penalty kick. Will he be able to score?

 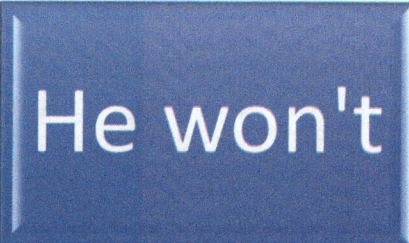

Did Lionel Messi score?

Lionel Messi misses from the penalty spot! The goalkeeper kicked the ball in front of him. Messi tried to head the ball into an empty net......

Once again, he missed the goal.

He gets 0 points. If you guessed the right answer and Lionel didn't score, you get 6 points.

Let's summarize the results of our game. Let's count the points.

The final table.

VS Lionel Messi

Players		**Lionel Messi**
1 round		3 points
2 round		2 points
3 round		3 points
4 round		0 points
5 round		3 points
6 round		3 points
7 round		0 points
Bottom line		14 points

Anyway, good for you! You played against one of the greatest players of all time! As you can see, even Messi didn't always make the right decisions, even the great ones make mistakes. The main thing is to practice, analyze and correct your mistakes. Good luck, champ!

Made in the USA
Coppell, TX
07 December 2023